CHILDREN'S LETTERS TO GOD

They're funny, they're touching, they're no-holds-barred honest—for when kids write to God they let it all hang out. From thousands of letters collected by Stuart Hample and Eric Marshall for their books and syndicated column, they have selected the cream of the crop.

Under "Requests—Reasonable and Otherwise" Bruce writes, "Dear God, Please send me a pony. I never asked for anything before. You can look it up."

Under "The Critics: Complaints, Warnings, Suggestions, Reservations and Doubts" we find an ultimatum from a little girl named Joy—"Dear God, If you don't take the baby back I will not clean up my room."

But God gets a lot of praise, too, as in this letter from Herbert: "Dear God, Count me in. Your friend, Herbie."

Serialized in *The Ladies' Home Journal* and *Reader's Digest* and a nationally syndicated column currently appearing in 128 newspapers across the country, CHILDREN'S LETTERS TO GOD has won millions of fans and was an NBC-TV Special.

CHiLDren's Letters TO GOD

Compiled by Eric Marshall and Stuart Hample

Illustrated by Stuart Hample

PUBLISHED BY POCKET BOOKS NEW YORK

CHILDREN'S LETTERS TO GOD

New enlarged POCKET BOOK edition published April, 1975

This POCKET BOOK edition is printed from brand-new plates made from completely reset, clear, easy-to-read type. POCKET BOOK editions are published by POCKET BOOKS, a division of Simon & Schuster, Inc., 630 Fifth Avenue, New York, N.Y. 10020. Trademarks registered in the United States and other countries.

Standard Book Number: 671-78874-4.

Front cover drawing by Stuart Hample.

Printed in the U.S.A.

1265

INTRODUCTION

The letters in this book express that part of a child's world reserved for special thoughts and wishes. Their subject matter ranges through those beliefs, desires, questions, and doubts that are urgent and common to all children. Some of them are disarmingly wise, others naïve, some knowing, some simple, some reverent, some not so reverent. Many are weighted with seriousness, others are lit with smiles. All of them are addressed to God with much hope and trust. Grownups know for certain, of course, that no matter how much postage they carry they will not get there—but then grownups know so much more than children—sometimes.

In choosing these letters, we have tried to convey, as much as possible, the incredible variety they represent. Spelling and grammar have not been corrected, for what they say they say better as they are.

—Eric Marshall and Stuart Hample

CONTENTS

REQUESTS

DEAR GOD,
I WOULD LIKE
THESE THINGS.
a new bicycle
a number three chemistry
set
a dog
a movie camera
a first base man glove

IF I CAN'T HAVE
THEM ALL I WOULD
LIKE TO HAVE MOST
OF THEM.

YOURS
TRULY
ERIC

P.S. I KNOW THERE
IS NO SANTA CLAUS

Please make
it so dogs live
as long as
people. Nancy

DEAR GOD, - MY FATHAR SAID KIDS IS THE BEST TIME IN LIFE. PLEASE TELL HIM WHAT GOOD IS IT IF WE NEVER GET TO STAY UP AND WATCH ANYTHING.

JO

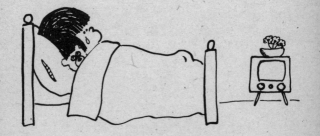

Dear Dear God
I Think iT is terrific
the way They got
The astronauts to go up
To go around around
the world. please dont
let it fall on our
house
        Your friend
        Norman

Dear Sir,
Can you
show me
how paint
comes off?

Howard

Dear God,
   I would like a duck next easter I am tired of the same thing every time o.k? Love.
            Margaret

Dear God,
    I would like
to be a snake
some times but
only when I
want.   Andy

Dear God.
I would like all the bad things to Stop.

Debbie

Dear God,
 I lost my glove
again and I'm going
to get heck unless
 somebody
sticks up for me.
Will you.
       MARTHA

Remembr when
the snow was so
deep there was
no school.
Could we
have it again

Guy

Dear God,
My father is mean.
Please get him not to be.
But don't hurt him.
Sincerly.
Martin

Dear God,
 My father can never get a fire started. Could you make a burning bush in our yard?
 Sherry

Instead of
die and haveing
ones   why dont

letting people

to make new

you just keep

the ones you

got now?

Jane

Dear God
Please send me
Pony. I never
askd for anything
before You can
look it up
                Bruce

OFFERS

Dear God,
O.K. I kept
my half of
the deal.
Where's
the bike.

Bert

Dear God
My Father is
very smart.
Maybe
he could
help You.

Margo

DEAR GOD. I MADE
26¢ SELLING LEMONADE
I WILL GIVE YOU
SOME OF IT ON SUNDAY

CHRIS

DEAR GOD
I AM SENDING
YOU A PENNY TO
GIVE A KID
POORER THAN ME
LOVE. DONNA

If you give me a genie lamp like Aladin, I will give you anything you want besids money or my chess set

Raphael

DEAR God

If you will make
it so I can be
invisible when I
want to I will do all
the things you want

Is it a deal?

Your Friend

Gordon

Dear God,
   If you send the
camera I will
send something
good to you
                    Peter

Dear God, I want to be a bird. If you will do it I promis not to ask for anything for a long time.

David.

THE CRITICS

If they don't want
you to make
your own break-
fast they
should say
So before

Timmy

Dear God
The people in the next apartment fight real loud all the time. You should only let very good friends get married.
Nan

Dear God,
I got left back.

Thanks alot

Raymond

DEAR GOD
HOW COME YOU
DIDN'T INVENT ANY
NEW ANIMALS LATELY?
WE STILL HAVE JUST
ALL THE OLD ONES

JOHNNY

Dear God,

I wished on a star
two times
but nothing
happened.

Now what?

Anna

Dear God,
   That fairy you sent
left 5¢ for my tooth
and a quarter for
my brother's. So you
still owe me 20¢.

        Peter.

Dear God,
  Are you real?
Some people
don't not believe
it. If you are
you better do
something quick.

Harriet Ann

Dear God,
If you don't take
the baby back I
will not clean up
my room.

Joy

Dear God,

Church is alright but you could sure use better music I hope this does not hurt your feeling.

Can you write some new songs

Your friend
Barry

Dear God
Do you always get
the right souls
in the right people.
you could make a
mistake.
                Cindy

ONE OF YOUR CLOUDS
MaDe A FACe THaT
ScaRed Me. PLeAse
DON'T DO it aGAin

Ellen

Dear God,

Christmas should

be earlier because

kids can only

be good
for so
long.

Beth

DEAR GOD
WHAT IS THE
USE OF BEING
GOOD IF
NO BODY
KNOWS IT
MARK

Dear God—
Please put a-
nother HOLiday
between Christmas
and EASTER.
There is nothing good
in there now.
    Ginny

Dear God
I went to this wedding and they kissed right in church. Is that O.K.

Neil

Why did you make so many People? Could you make another earth and put the extras there.
J.B.

CONFESSIONS

Dear God,

Don't Listen To My Solo until Satar-day, Please

Love,

Beth

Dear God
When you make
a miracel every-
body says it is
great, but I can't
even play a trick
without getting it.
                    Allison

Dear God, I hope ants not special be-cause we squish them all the time.

Dennis

DEAR GOD

I KNOW YOU ARE SUP-OSED TO LOVE THY NEIGHBER BUT IF MARK KEEPS TAKEING MY OTHER SKATE HE'S GOING TO GET IT

KEVIN

Dear God,
   A lot of People
     say bad things
with your name in it
but I never do.

                    Helen

Dear, God I am sorry for the bad things I did when I was little.

Peter F

DEAR GOD
I TRY TO BE LIKE GEORGE
WASHINGTON AND NEVER
LIE BUT SOMÉTIMS I
MISS   RALPH

Dear God,
I am doing the
best I can.
Frank

Dear God,
 I would like to be
a Doctor But not
for the Reason
you think.   Ferd.

Dear God.
I want to be a
inventor but I
don't know what
to invent.
                    Carl

I SORRY DID NOT
WRITE BEFORE
BUT I ONLY
LEARNED HOW
THIS WEEK

MARTHA

AGE
5

Dear God,
Donald broke
the jar NOT me
Now you
have it
in writing

Jane

Dear God
We got a lot of
religion in our
house. So dont
worry about
us.   Teddy

INCIDENTAL
INFORMATION

Dear God
  Yesterday I had pizza for luch and spogetie and meat bulls for dinner. What did you have?

Anne Marie

Dear God,

I have been reading all the things that happened long ago. When the sun stood still and David and °Goliath and Daniel with the lions den and the story of Ruth and the fall of Jericho. A lot of things happend in your days.

Yours trully,

Joe.

Dear God,

I ~~have~~ pictures
of all the
leaders except
you.

Norman

Dear God,
I would like to be a teacher so so I can boss people around.

Jennifer

DEar GOD
NOBODY WANTS
tO BE YOUR
BUDDY WHEN
YOUR FAt

Martha

Dear God
I have to know
who Shakespeare
is before next
Friday.
          Melissa

Dear, God,
   I remember
when you were
a baby, You
were **b**orn in
a manger
                 Brenda

AGE-7

I can see
The Sun

Laura Moffitt

Dear God

I Love You God.

during arithmetic

a dog came in.

Krista

Dear God
I want to
get married
but no-one
will do it
with me
yet.   Dody

Dear Dad,
Mrs Coe got
a new
refrigrartr. We
got the box it
came in for a
club house.
So thats where
I will be if you
are looking
for me.

Marvin

The Jewish peopel
sellabrat 16 Jewish
Holiday's. One of
the Holiday's are
Chanakah.

Debbie

Dear God,
   On Holloween I
am going to wear
a Devil's Costume.
Is that all right
with You?
              Marnie

EARNEST INQUIRIES

Dear God

Is mother natur in your family.

Linda 3B

Dear God,
When you made
The first man
did he work as
good as we

do now.

Tom

Dear God,

Can you

marry

food?

Martha

Dear God

Where does everybody come from? I hope you explain it better than my father.

Ward

Dear Mr. God,
How do you feel
about people who
don't believe in
you? Somebody
else wants to
know.

a friend,
neil

Dear God
Did you
mean for
giraffe to
look like
that or
was it an
accident

Norma

DEAR GOD
ARE THERE ANY
PATRIARCHS
AROUND TODAY
PATRICK

How did you know you were God?

Charlene

Dear God,
      When you
make it rain
how do you
know how
long to do it.
            Terry

Who draws the
lines around
the countries?
Nan

Dear God
Are you
rich or just
famous.

Steven

Dear God,
Do plastic
flowers make you
mad? I would
be if I made the
real ones.

Lucy

AUTHOR, AUTHOR!

Dear God
In bible times
did they
really talk
that fancy

Norma

Dear God

I got this new bible and your name is in "it.

Love Teddy

DEAR GOD
DID YOU MAKE
PEOPLE OR
ANIMAL FIRST?
IT DOESN'T SAY
SO ANY PLACE.

RUPERT
AGE 9

WHY ISNT' MRS. GODS
NAME IN THE BIBBLE
? WERENT' YOU
MARRIED TO HER WHEN
YOU WROTE IT?
LARRY

Dear God,
  I read your book.
I like it verry
much. It is called
the Bible.   Love,
           Maggie

Dear God,

Could you write more stories. We have already read all the ones you have and begin again.

Gratefully,

Emily

Dear God

If it is in The Bible it is true isnt it? like in the encyclopedia

Gene
Age 9

I read your
book and I
like it.
where do you
get your
Ideas
John P.

Dear God,
I think the
BIBLE is very
good. Did you
write any
other books?
ALICE

IF YOU'RE
SO SMART

If you are so smart
let's see if you can read
my code:

VDDL RBT CLJKS
NT PSD KLHSM
ATFO

If you can read it,
make it rain tomorrow
so I will know.

Gabe

Dear God -
If we had fur
like the animals
we wouldn't have
to wear clothes.
Did you ever
think of that?

Wally W.

Dear

What are

Rodd W

IF YOU DON'T WANT
PEOPLE TO SAY BAD
WORDS WHY DID YOU
INVENT THEM?
EUGENE

Dear God
I know it says
turn the other
cheek but what
if your sister hit
you on the eye.
Love
Teresa

Dear God
Why
does
trees
Grow
tall and
pepole Grow
littel
GARY

Dear God
    Why don't you Leave the sun out at night when we need it the most.
        Barbara.

I am seven years old.

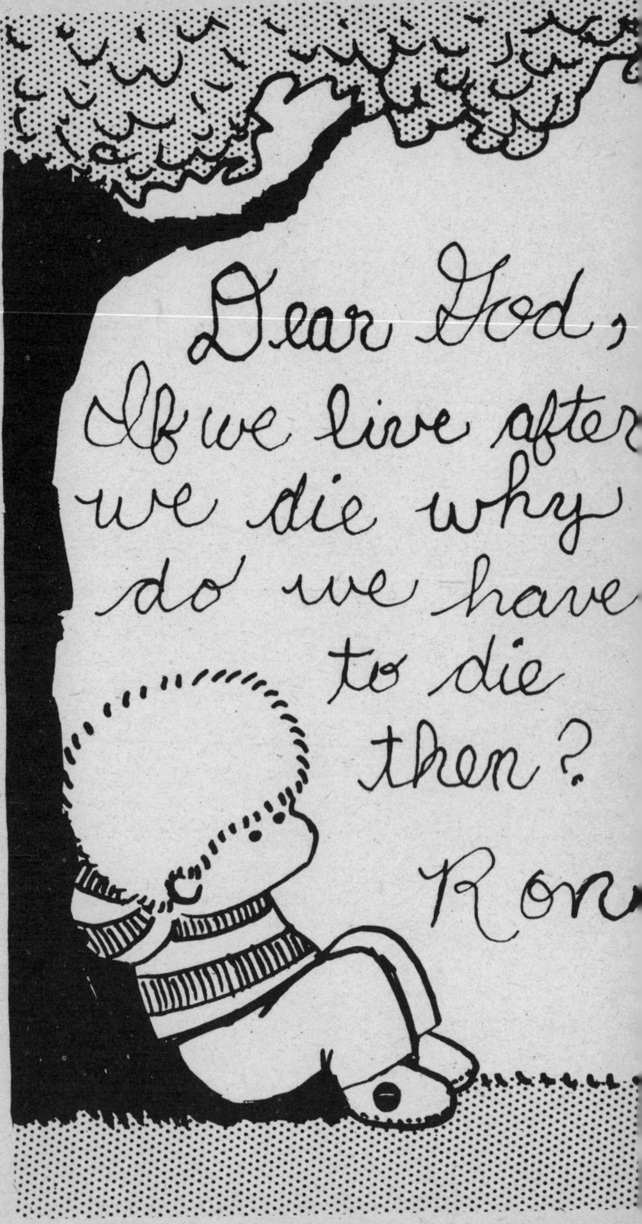
Dear God,
If we live after
we die why
do we have
to die
then?
Ron

We read Thos.
Edison made
light. I thought
you did that.
            Donna.

Dear God
My teacher
the north pole
the top. Did You
mistakes?

Says
's not really at
make any other

Herbie

Dear God
   Why do I
have to pray
wen You know
anyway what I
want? But I'll
do it if it makes
You feel better.

         Sue

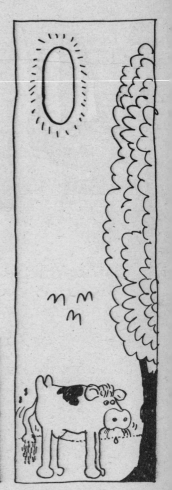

Dear God - My
teacher says the
days get shorter
then they get
longer. Cant'
you decide?

Mindy

Why did you make the sky blue and the grass green. Is that the only colors you got?

PRAISE

Dear God,

Count me in

Your friend

Herbie

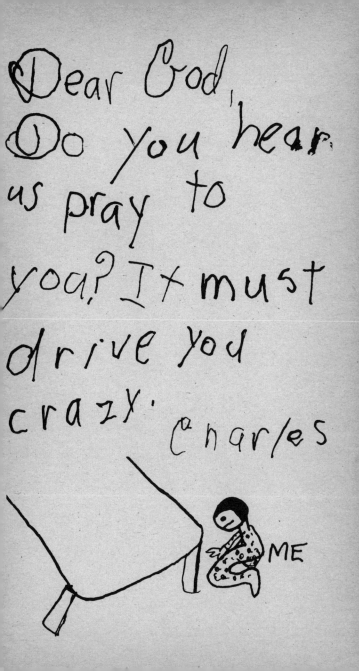

YOU arE
ONE OF MY
two
FarOritE
MEN IN tHE
WORLd

Patti

Dear God,
Last week it rained
three days. We thought
it would be like
Noah's Ark. but it
wasn't. I'm glad
because you could
only take two of things,
remember, and we
have three cats.

Donna

Dear God,
Did you
think up
hugging?
That is a
good thing.

Brenda

Dear God,
I want to be just
like you when I am
your age.
O.K?
Tommy

Dear God,
It's very good the way each kid has one mother and one father. Did it take you long to think of that? Glenn

Dear God
If I was
God I
wouldn't
be as good
at it. Keep
it up.
Michelle

DEAR GOD
I LIKE HOW YOU
MADE DOGS IN
DIFFERENT FLAVORS
JUDY

Dear God,
  I saw Saint Patrick church last week when we went to New York.

You live in a nice house

                    Frank

Dear God
If you let dinasor not exstinct we
would not have a country!
You did the right thing. Jonathan

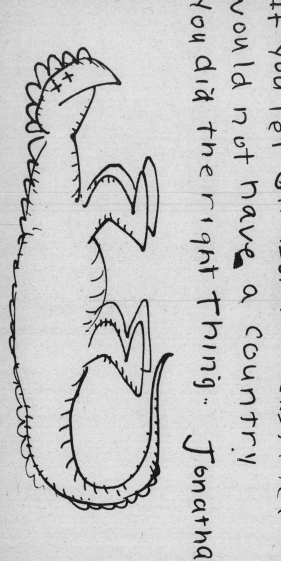

Dear God.
If you made
the sun the moon

& stars you
must of had lots
of equipment.

Paul

Dear God,
When I wake
up I am
glad you left
every thing
right where it
was

chris

Dear God—
I didn't' think
orange went very
good with purple
until I saw the
sunset you made on
Tue. That was cool.
Eugene

STUART HAMPLE, who co-edited this book with Eric Marshall, and also illustrated it, is the author of numerous books for children. His picture books include *Mr. Nobody And The Umbrella Bug*, *Doodles The Deer-Horse*, and *The Silly Book*, which was turned into a Columbia record with lyrics by Mr. Hample. Mr. Hample has written and performed for children on television, too, as host of "The Crayon Man" over New York's Channel 13, as a guest on "Captain Kangaroo," and as writer of a number of specials, among which was "Children's Letters To God," an adaptation of his best-selling book for NBC-TV, featuring Gene Kelly. He continues to collect letters from children, along with Mr. Marshall, for his syndicated newspaper feature, "Children's Letters," which appears in papers throughout the country. His own children range in age from 11 to 18 and are, he notes sadly, now too old to give him inspiration for his books.